THIS COLORING BOOK BELONGS TO:

For more coloring adventures,
please scan the QR Codes:

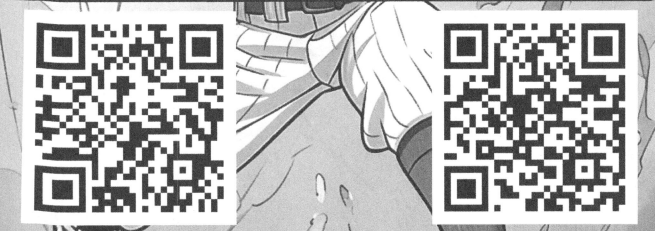

If you enjoyed this book, please kindly leave a review.
This helps us to make more fun books for you.

THANK YOU

If you enjoyed this book, please kindly leave a review.
This helps us to produce more books for you.

YOU MAY ALSO LIKE:

ANIMAL WORD SEARCH PUZZLE BOOK

FUN FACTS FOR KIDS

CRUISE JOURNAL FOR WOMEN: Capturing Memories at Sea.

ANXIETY RELIEF: KICK THAT ANXIETY BUTT: Stop Worrying and Get Over It.

SCAN
QR CODE

Made in the USA
Monee, IL
19 November 2024

70552078R00063